EGYPTIAN MYTHS

Kathy Elgin

Skyview
Books
an imprint of

WINDMILL
BOOKS
New York

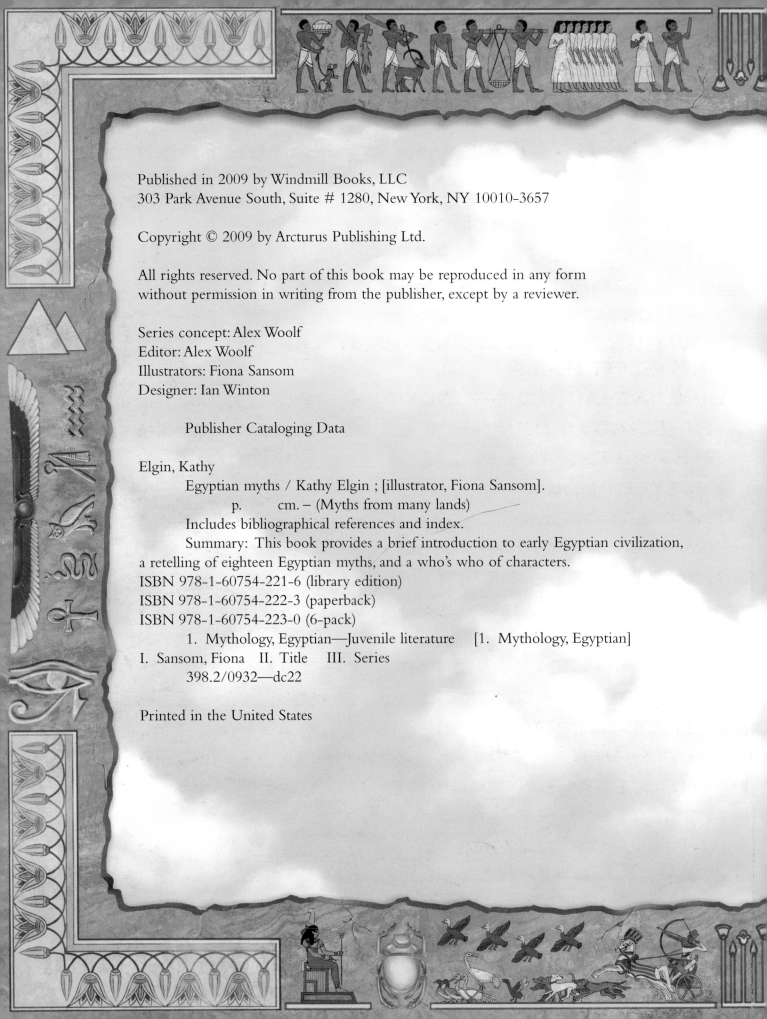

Published in 2009 by Windmill Books, LLC
303 Park Avenue South, Suite # 1280, New York, NY 10010-3657

Series concept: Alex Woolf
Editor: Alex Woolf
Illustrators: Fiona Sansom
Designer: Ian Winton

        Publisher Cataloging Data

Elgin, Kathy
        Egyptian myths / Kathy Elgin ; [illustrator, Fiona Sansom].
               p.   cm. – (Myths from many lands)
        Includes bibliographical references and index.
        Summary: This book provides a brief introduction to early Egyptian civilization,
a retelling of eighteen Egyptian myths, and a who's who of characters.
ISBN 978-1-60754-221-6 (library edition)
ISBN 978-1-60754-222-3 (paperback)
ISBN 978-1-60754-223-0 (6-pack)
        1. Mythology, Egyptian—Juvenile literature   [1. Mythology, Egyptian]
I. Sansom, Fiona   II. Title   III. Series
        398.2/0932—dc22

Printed in the United States

CONTENTS

INTRODUCTION

Egypt was one of the world's first great civilizations. It began almost 5,000 years ago and lasted over 3,000 years.

POWERFUL PHARAOHS

Egypt was ruled by families of kings, or pharaohs. It was the tradition for the pharaoh to marry his sister, so that power stayed in the family. The first pharaoh was Menes, who built his capital city at Memphis. People believed that their most powerful pharaohs were divine. They worshipped them as gods, even while they were alive.

GODS AND GODDESSES

The Egyptians also worshipped many other gods. We know what they looked like because they made statues of their gods and painted their pictures on the walls of tombs.

MEDITERRANEAN SEA

GIZA •• MEMPHIS

NILE

EGYPT

RED SEA

• THEBES

N
W E
S

Some gods had more than one name. Some had more than one personality. They could be wicked and kind at the same time. Sometimes, over hundreds of years, two gods were combined into one. There are also different versions of the same story. This can be quite confusing!

SAILORS AND WARRIORS

The Egyptians were curious and energetic people. Most were farmers, but they were also the first people to build seagoing boats. They traveled huge distances. Egyptian armies conquered other tribes and created a great empire.

THE STRONG AND THE WEAK

Egyptian society was organized in layers of importance. A diagram would look like one of their pyramids, with the pharaoh at the top. Underneath him came his family. Next came the priests, then scribes or scholars, then soldiers, craftsmen, and farmers. On the very bottom layer were slaves and servants.

THE END

Ramses III was the last great pharaoh. The rulers who followed him were weak. This allowed foreign armies to invade the country. In 300 BC, Alexander the Great conquered Egypt. He founded a dynasty of Greek pharaohs called the Ptolemies. The famous queen Cleopatra was the last of these. When she died in 30 BC, Egypt became part of the Roman Empire. The great civilization was over.

HOW RA CREATED THE WORLD

When time first began, the world was covered with water and darkness. There was nothing to see or hear. Then, out of the dark waters, a big shining egg appeared, and out of it came the great god Ra. He was so powerful that he created things just by giving them a name.

First he spoke the name of Shu, the god of air, and the first winds blew. Then he created Tefnut, the goddess of moisture, and the first rain fell. Next, Ra created Geb, god of the earth, and Nut, goddess of the sky. Nut's body made an enormous arch over the earth, with her hands and feet touching the ground.

Then Ra created Hapi, god of the Nile, and the great river began to flow, making the land rich and fertile. When everything was ready, Ra created the animals and birds and, last of all, men and women.

Ra became the first pharaoh and reigned on earth for many centuries.

THE BENNU BIRD

The bennu bird was the first creature named by Ra. It perched on a mound of earth sticking out of the dark water and gave a loud cry. With this, time began, and the hours, weeks, and years were created.

The bennu's perch became a sacred place called Heliopolis. This means "city of the sun."

After many centuries, the bennu grew old. It built a nest of sacred twigs and breathed fire onto them. As the nest burned, a new, young bennu flew out from the flames. Life began again.

HOW THOTH OVERCAME THE CURSE OF RA

Ra was afraid that one day a child of the goddess Nut would overthrow him. He put a curse on Nut, preventing her from having a child on any day of the year.

Full of sorrow, Nut asked Thoth, god of wisdom, for help. As usual, Thoth had a clever idea. He went to Khonsu, the moon god, and challenged him to a game of checkers. They played game after game, but Thoth always won.

As the stakes grew higher and higher, Khonsu became angry. He began to bet his precious moonlight against Thoth. This was just what Thoth wanted.

At last, Khonsu had to admit defeat. Thoth gathered up all the light he had won and made it into five extra days. He set these between the end of the old year and the beginning of the new one. Because these five days did not belong to either year, Nut was able to have a child on each one of them.

She gave birth first to Osiris, then his wicked brother Seth. They were followed by Isis, her younger sister Nephthys, and finally Horus. He was later known as Horus the Elder because his famous nephew had the same name.

But poor Khonsu did not have enough moonlight left to shine brightly every night. So, ever since that time, the moon waxes and wanes throughout the month.

THE STORY OF THE RED DRINK

(OR HOW RA PUNISHED MANKIND)

Over the years, men and women lost respect for Ra. They started to break his laws and commit wicked deeds. Ra saw all this and decided to punish mankind. He sent his daughter Sekhmet to teach them a lesson.

Sekhmet turned herself into a lion and ran through the country killing men, women, and children, and eating them. The river Nile ran red with their blood.

Eventually Ra took pity, but even he was unable to stop Sekhmet. By now, she loved the taste of blood.

Ra commanded the women of Egypt to brew a strong drink and mix it with red powder to resemble blood. When they had brewed seven thousand jars of the red drink, they poured it over the land. Thinking it was blood, Sekhmet drank it up until she was so dizzy she could no longer kill people.

After this, Sekhmet changed her name to Hathor. She became famous for her love and compassion.

HOW ISIS TRICKED RA INTO REVEALING HIS SECRET NAME

Because he had become human, eventually the great Ra grew old. His body was bent, and he trembled and dribbled like old men do.

Isis, the clever daughter of Nut and Geb, wanted to gain Ra's great power for herself. She knew that she could only do this by learning the secret name that only Ra himself knew.

Next time her grandfather dribbled spit, Isis mixed it with mud and made a snake out of it. Shortly afterward, Ra passed by and the snake bit him. Ra was in great pain. He could not understand how one of his own creatures could hurt him. But of course he had not created that serpent.

Isis, who was the goddess of healing, agreed to cure him with a magic spell. But, she said, she needed Ra's secret name for the spell to work.

Ra grew worse. Eventually he had to tell Isis his name, but he made her swear never to reveal it to anyone but her son Horus.

HOW RA TRAVELED THE SKIES IN HIS GREAT BOAT

After Isis had taken away his power, Ra recovered, but he was no longer able to reign on earth as pharaoh. Instead, he took a new place in the heavens.

Every day, Ra traveled across the sky in his sacred golden boat. This boat was so bright and shining that Ra became known as the sun god. People watched him sail across the sky, lighting up the day and bringing warmth to the world.

At night he traveled through the underworld, and during this time the earth was dark. In the underworld Ra faced many dangerous monsters. The worst of these was a terrible dragon called Apep. Every night Ra fought a battle with Apep but always managed to defeat him.

Every day, Ra collected the souls of people who had died and took them with him in his boat, to be judged in the underworld.

The people got used to Ra's journeys. They started to call these times "day" and "night."

THE LEGEND OF OSIRIS

Osiris, the grandson of Ra, married his sister Isis in the traditional way. Together they ruled Egypt in peace for many years. Their brother Seth, however, was envious and planned to kill Osiris.

Seth commanded his carpenters to make a magic box, exactly the size and shape of Osiris. During a feast, Seth tricked his brother into getting inside it, then sealed the box so that Osiris could not get out. Osiris died and Seth threw the box into the River Nile so that it floated far away.

Now that Seth was pharaoh, terrible times came to Egypt. Crops did not grow, animals died, and the people became greedy and wicked.

Queen Isis had been banished from court. In disguise, she went in search of the body of Osiris. After many long journeys she found it and brought it back to Egypt. She asked Thoth to help bring Osiris back to life. But before Thoth could work his magic, Seth discovered their plan. He stole the body and tore it into fourteen pieces.

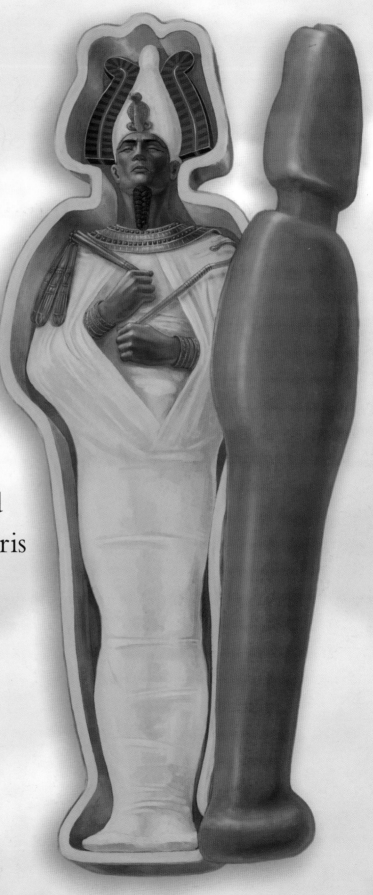

Seth scattered the pieces far and wide, hoping that crocodiles would eat them. But brave Isis searched again and eventually found all but one piece.

Between them, Thoth and Anubis, god of death, put the body back together and created a new limb to replace the missing one. Osiris lived again, but because he had been brought back from the dead, he could no longer live on earth. He became god of the underworld, where he watched over the souls of the dead.

SETH AND THE STONE BOAT

When Horus, son of Isis and Osiris, grew up, he wanted to avenge his father's murder and win the crown for himself.

He challenged his wicked uncle Seth to a race in stone boats. Of course, Seth's boat sank at once. Clever Horus, however, made his boat of wood painted to look like stone. He won the race, and Seth was banished to the skies to become god of storms.

But Seth was not all wicked. He rowed Ra's sacred boat at night and protected him from the evil monsters in the underworld.

THE EYE OF HORUS

During one of their many battles, Seth tore out Horus's left eye. He ripped it into tiny pieces and scattered them into the sea.

Thoth found the pieces and gave them back to Horus. He managed to put his eye back together again, but it was never as strong as the right eye. When Horus looked over the earth, his strong right eye was like the sun. The weaker left eye was like the moon, shining less brightly.

The Eye of Horus is still a powerful symbol of healing in Egypt.

THE GREAT BATTLE BETWEEN SETH AND HORUS

Queen Isis had given birth to Horus by magic, after Seth had killed her husband Osiris. When Horus was a little boy, Isis had hidden him away on a secret island because she had always known that Seth would try to harm him.

Somehow Seth had found out where the child was. Seth sent demons and monsters to kill Horus. However, Horus was protected by strong magic and all these attacks had failed.

Often, the spirit of his dead father Osiris had visited Horus to give him advice. Now he was a strong and brave young man. In spite of all Seth's tricks, Horus was not afraid of him.

After the contest of the stone boats, they met for a last great battle on the Nile. Seth could turn himself into any animal he chose. First he took the form of a black boar but this did not frighten Horus. Next he turned himself into a huge red hippopotamus and raised a thunderstorm to wreck Horus's ship.

Horus took the form of a handsome giant,

over ten feet (three meters) tall. He held a
mighty harpoon, and with one stroke he killed
the hippopotamus. It sank beneath the waves and
all the people cheered.

So Horus finally defeated his wicked uncle. But
their spirits continued to be at war. When Seth
was winning, times were bad. But when Horus
had the upper hand, the world was peaceful.

Legend says that at
the end of time, Horus
will defeat Seth in one
final battle and Osiris
will return from the
underworld.

THE WEIGHING OF THE HEART AND THE FEATHER

When someone died, the soul, or ka, went down to the underworld for judgment. Thoth led the ka to where Osiris sat on his throne. In front of Osiris stood a huge balance with two scales. Thoth stood waiting to record the judgment in his great book.

The ka had to declare that it had led a good life. Then Anubis, god of death, took out the heart and placed it on one of the scales. In the other scale was a feather, the symbol of truth. This was the moment people feared most. If the heart was lighter than the feather, the soul was truthful. Osiris nodded and the ka passed on to the Fields of Peace.

But if the heart was heavier than the feather, the person had been sinful. Ammit the Devourer of Hearts was waiting to grab the heart and eat it. Sinful souls were thrown into the Pits of Fire where the dragon Apep lived. This was a terrible fate.

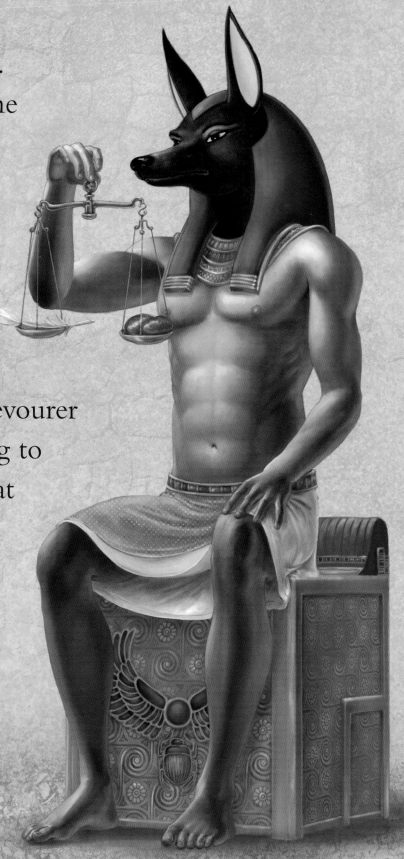

THE BOY WHO READ THE SEALED LETTER

Se-Osiris – his name means "Gift of Osiris" – was the most clever child in all Egypt. He was just twelve years old, but he had amazing magical powers. One day an Ethiopian arrived at the pharaoh's court. He challenged all the magicians of Egypt to read the contents of a sealed letter without opening it.

Se-Osiris read the letter easily. It said that Ethiopian magic was stronger than Egyptian magic. The magician was furious at being beaten. He conjured up a huge snake to threaten the pharaoh. Se-Osiris just laughed and pointed at the snake. Immediately it shrank to a small white worm. Se-Osiris picked it up and threw it out of the window.

Next, the Ethopian called up a cloud of darkness. Se-Osiris rolled it into a ball and threw it away. Finally, the magician conjured a wall of fire. Se-Osiris blew on the flames so they wrapped around the magician. All that was left was a pile of ash. "So," said Se-Osiris, "whose magic is stronger?"

KING THUTMOSE AND THE SPHINX

The pharaoh had many sons, but Prince Thutmose was his favorite. Thutmose's brothers were jealous of this and were always plotting against him.

This made Thutmose unhappy. He spent his time out in the desert hunting alone. One day he found himself near the great pyramids at Giza. Sticking out of the sand nearby was part of a giant statue. It had the body of a lion and the head of a pharaoh and wore the royal crown of Egypt. It was a sphinx.

Suddenly, the statue spoke to him. "I am your ancestor, Harmachis, god of the rising sun. If you clear the sand away from my resting place, I will protect you and make you a great king."

Thutmose fell to the ground in a daze. When he awoke he swore to do what the sphinx had asked. He sent servants to clear away the sand. Very soon after that he was made heir to the throne and became one of Egypt's greatest rulers.

THE GOLDEN LOTUS

Pharaoh Seneferu was bored. He ordered his chief magician Zazamankh to entertain him. Zazamankh suggested a sailing trip. He provided a beautiful boat, rowed by twenty beautiful maidens. Each one was dressed in cloth of gold and wore a gold headdress shaped like a lotus flower.

Suddenly, one of the girls' headdresses fell into the water and sank. She wept and refused to be comforted. Seneferu again called for Zazamankh. "Watch," said the magician, "and I will show you something wonderful."

Zazamankh touched the water with his wand. At once the water began to part. The little boat sank down until they found themselves on the dry bottom of the lake. High walls of water towered on either side. Right beside them was the golden lotus. The girl picked it up and skipped happily back into the boat.

With another stroke of his wand, Zazamankh brought the water together again. Soon the little boat was back on the surface as if nothing had happened. But Seneferu was no longer bored.

THE GIRL WITH THE ROSE-RED SLIPPERS
(A CINDERELLA STORY)

A wealthy Greek merchant called Charaxos lived in Egypt. One day in the slave market he saw a beautiful girl called Rhodopis, which means "rosy cheeks." He knew she was Greek, like him. He bought her, and treated her like his own daughter.

Of all the lovely things he gave her, her favorite was a pair of rose-red slippers. One day, when she was bathing in the pool, an eagle swooped down. It picked up one of her slippers and flew away over the valley.

When it came to the royal palace, it flew down and dropped the slipper into the pharaoh's lap. He looked at the pretty slipper. He thought its owner must also be very beautiful. He sent messengers out to search the land.

Eventually they came to Charaxos's house. Rhodopis was surprised to see her slipper again, and even more surprised when she arrived at the royal palace. The pharaoh was sure that the gods had sent her and at once made Rhodopis his queen.

THE STORY OF THE SHIPWRECKED SAILOR

A sailor came to the pharaoh's court with a wonderful story to tell. He had been shipwrecked alone on a mysterious island. Suddenly, he heard a terrible noise. There in front of him was a giant snake, covered in golden scales and with eyes like jewels.

The snake picked him up in its jaws and carried him to a cave. "This island is the kingdom of serpents," said the snake. "You have been sent by the gods to visit us. At the end of four months you will be rescued, so that you can tell your great pharaoh about us."

The sailor promised to do this, and also to return with gifts. The Snake King told him that no one could ever return to the island.

The sailor lived content for four months, eating the island's delicious fruit and fish. Then a rescue boat appeared. He got in, carrying gifts from the Snake King. But when he looked back, the island had vanished into thin air.

THE ADVENTURES OF SINUHE

One day a pharaoh was murdered. Sinuhe was his bodyguard. He had not been involved in the plot, but he knew people would suspect him, so he ran away.

After many long travels, he arrived in the land of Retenu. The king welcomed him and made him his adviser. Sinuhe became a powerful and wealthy man. He married the king's daughter and eventually became king himself.

Sinuhe grew old and he longed to see Egypt once more before he died. He wrote to the pharaoh, begging to be forgiven for running away. The pharaoh agreed at once. Sinuhe gave up his crown and all his wealth and set out for Egypt.

The pharaoh welcomed him like a son. He gave him back all the land and possessions he had left behind many years ago.

And so, after all, Sinuhe became a great man in Egypt. All the stories of his adventures were carved on his tomb when he died. And this is how we know his story.

THE TREASURE THIEF

When Pharaoh Ramses III had his great treasure house built, the clever builder put in a secret passage. Every night the builder's sons crept in and stole some of the treasure.

The pharaoh knew someone was stealing his treasure. He set a trap, and one of the brothers was caught. The other one cut off his brother's head so that the body could not be recognized. Later, he tricked the guards into letting him take the body away for burial.

The angry pharaoh set another trap. Disguised as a foreign princess, his daughter vowed to marry the man who confessed to the most clever and most wicked deeds.

The brother told the princess about the two things he had done. At once, soldiers jumped out and grabbed him by the arm. But they found they were holding a false arm! The thief had seen through the trick and escaped again.

The pharaoh laughed so much at the treasure thief's cleverness that he forgave him. And when he married the pharaoh's daughter, he no longer needed to steal.

WHO'S WHO IN EGYPTIAN MYTHS

ANUBIS

The god of the dead and of embalming lives in the underworld. He has the head of a black jackal, with pointed ears.

HORUS

He has many forms but is often shown as a child sucking his thumb, with his hair in a sidelock to symbolize youth. Sometimes he appears as a man with the head of a falcon, wearing the crowns of Upper and Lower Egypt. God of kingship, government, and good administration, he also looks after children and the pharaoh.

ISIS

Sister and wife of Osiris, Isis is often shown as a beautiful woman in a close-fitting dress. She wears a crown that looks like a throne with a sundisc behind her head. She is the goddess and protector of women and children.

OSIRIS

Grandson of Ra, Osiris is chief god of the underworld. Because he returned from the dead, he is shown wrapped in white graveclothes, like a mummy. To show that he was previously god of farming and vegetation, he has green skin and carries a shepherd's crook and a flail for threshing corn.

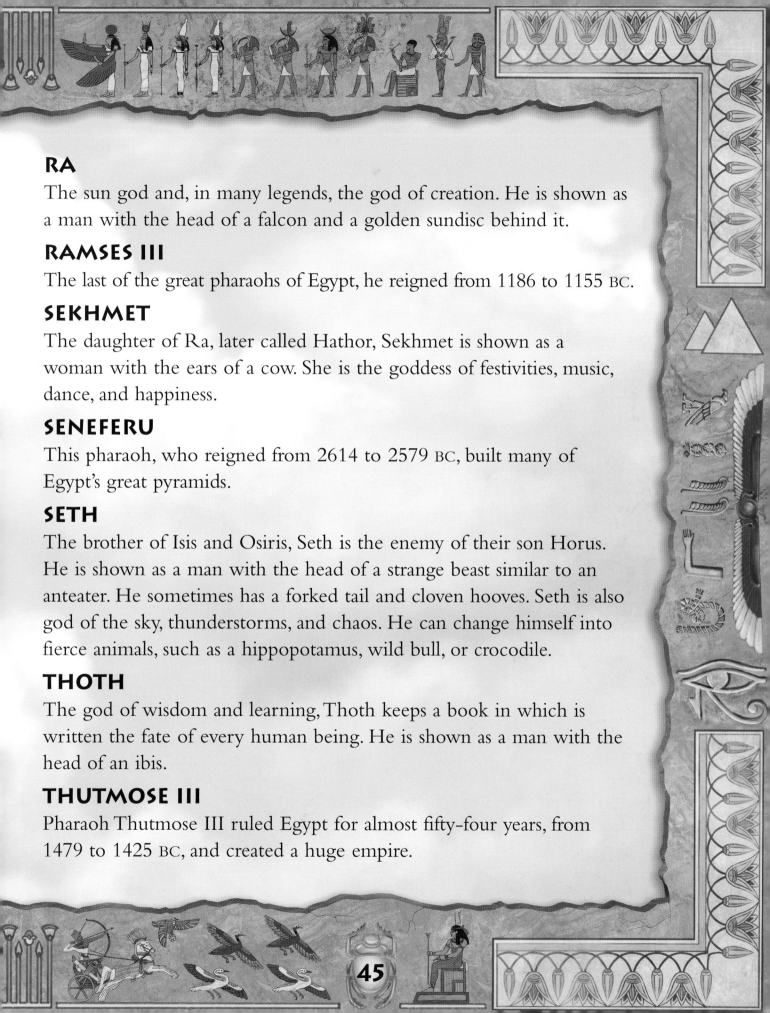

RA

The sun god and, in many legends, the god of creation. He is shown as a man with the head of a falcon and a golden sundisc behind it.

RAMSES III

The last of the great pharaohs of Egypt, he reigned from 1186 to 1155 BC.

SEKHMET

The daughter of Ra, later called Hathor, Sekhmet is shown as a woman with the ears of a cow. She is the goddess of festivities, music, dance, and happiness.

SENEFERU

This pharaoh, who reigned from 2614 to 2579 BC, built many of Egypt's great pyramids.

SETH

The brother of Isis and Osiris, Seth is the enemy of their son Horus. He is shown as a man with the head of a strange beast similar to an anteater. He sometimes has a forked tail and cloven hooves. Seth is also god of the sky, thunderstorms, and chaos. He can change himself into fierce animals, such as a hippopotamus, wild bull, or crocodile.

THOTH

The god of wisdom and learning, Thoth keeps a book in which is written the fate of every human being. He is shown as a man with the head of an ibis.

THUTMOSE III

Pharaoh Thutmose III ruled Egypt for almost fifty-four years, from 1479 to 1425 BC, and created a huge empire.

GLOSSARY

ancestor Somebody from whom a person is descended.

bodyguard A soldier who protects an important person.

chariot A light cart pulled by horses.

compassion Pity.

dynasty A sequence of rulers, usually from one family.

embalming Preserving a dead body in preparation for the afterlife by removing the internal organs and treating it with special herbs.

empire A group of peoples or countries under the control of a single ruler.

falcon A bird of prey.

fertile Capable of producing plentiful crops.

hieroglyph Egyptian picture writing. The name means 'sacred writing' in Greek.

hippopotamus A large animal that lives in African rivers.

ibis A wading bird with a long, curved beak.

jackal A kind of African dog with pointed ears and muzzle.

ka Part of the soul, usually shown as a version of a person's body.

lotus A kind of water lily.

nomads Wandering people of the desert.

papyrus A reed used for making paper. It is also the word for the paper itself.

pharaoh An Egyptian king.

pyramid A huge stone tomb with a square base and four sloping triangular sides.

scribe A person who could read and write and who recorded events.

serpent A snake.

sphinx A creature with a human head and a lion's body.

symbol Something that represents something else.

tomb A monument in which dead people are buried.

underworld A region below the earth where the souls of the dead go.

waxes and wanes Gets larger and then smaller (of the moon).

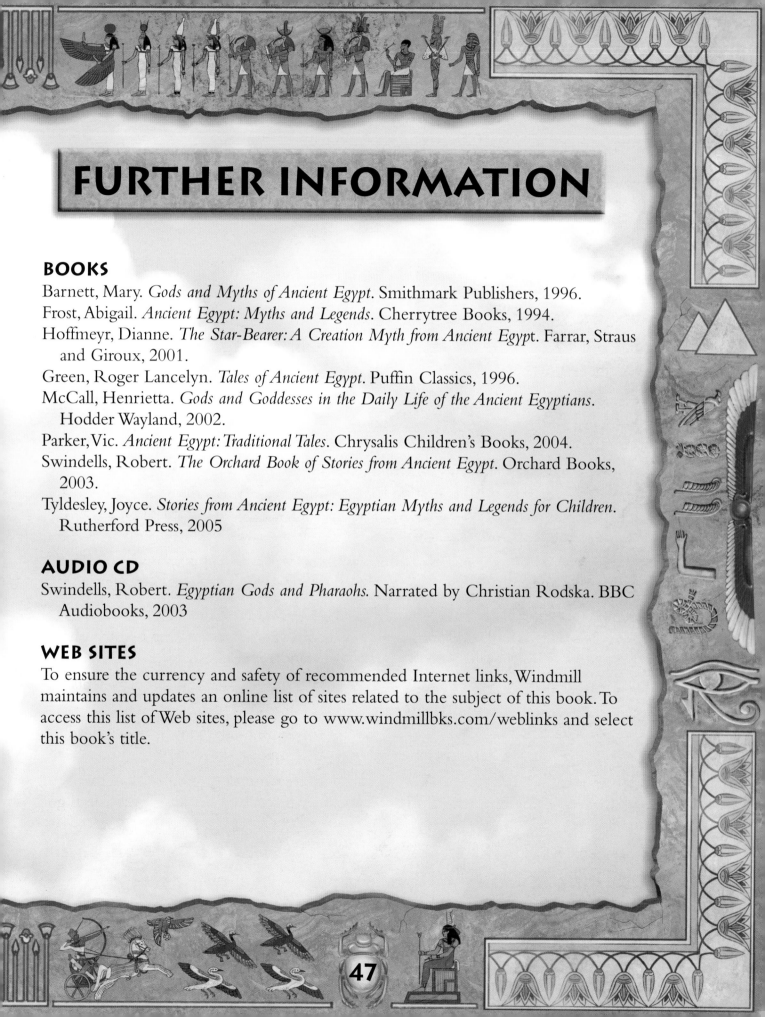

FURTHER INFORMATION

BOOKS

Barnett, Mary. *Gods and Myths of Ancient Egypt*. Smithmark Publishers, 1996.

Frost, Abigail. *Ancient Egypt: Myths and Legends*. Cherrytree Books, 1994.

Hoffmeyr, Dianne. *The Star-Bearer: A Creation Myth from Ancient Egypt*. Farrar, Straus and Giroux, 2001.

Green, Roger Lancelyn. *Tales of Ancient Egypt*. Puffin Classics, 1996.

McCall, Henrietta. *Gods and Goddesses in the Daily Life of the Ancient Egyptians*. Hodder Wayland, 2002.

Parker, Vic. *Ancient Egypt: Traditional Tales*. Chrysalis Children's Books, 2004.

Swindells, Robert. *The Orchard Book of Stories from Ancient Egypt*. Orchard Books, 2003.

Tyldesley, Joyce. *Stories from Ancient Egypt: Egyptian Myths and Legends for Children*. Rutherford Press, 2005

AUDIO CD

Swindells, Robert. *Egyptian Gods and Pharaohs*. Narrated by Christian Rodska. BBC Audiobooks, 2003

WEB SITES

To ensure the currency and safety of recommended Internet links, Windmill maintains and updates an online list of sites related to the subject of this book. To access this list of Web sites, please go to www.windmillbks.com/weblinks and select this book's title.

INDEX

For more great fiction and nonfiction, go to windmillbks.com.